MELODY BOBER

Romantic Rhapsodies

BOOK 2

Notes from the Publisher

Composers In Focus is a series of original piano collections celebrating the creative artistry of contemporary composers. It is through the work of these composers that the piano teaching repertoire is enlarged and enhanced.

It is my hope that students, teachers, and all others who experience this music will be enriched and inspired.

Frank J. Hackinson

Frank J. Hackinson, Publisher

Notes from the Composer

The elegance of a moonlit garden…the luster of an autumn sky…waltzing in a December snowfall…all of these conjure up images of romance in our mind's eye. As in Book 1, this collection features intermediate/late-intermediate solos with romantic themes designed to develop interpretation skills and expressive playing.

I hope you enjoy this book, and I wish you many romantic musical moments!

Sincerely,

Melody Bober

Melody Bober

Contents

Morning Dove

Melody Bober

6

Broadly

December Waltz

Flowing (♩ = ca. 152)

8

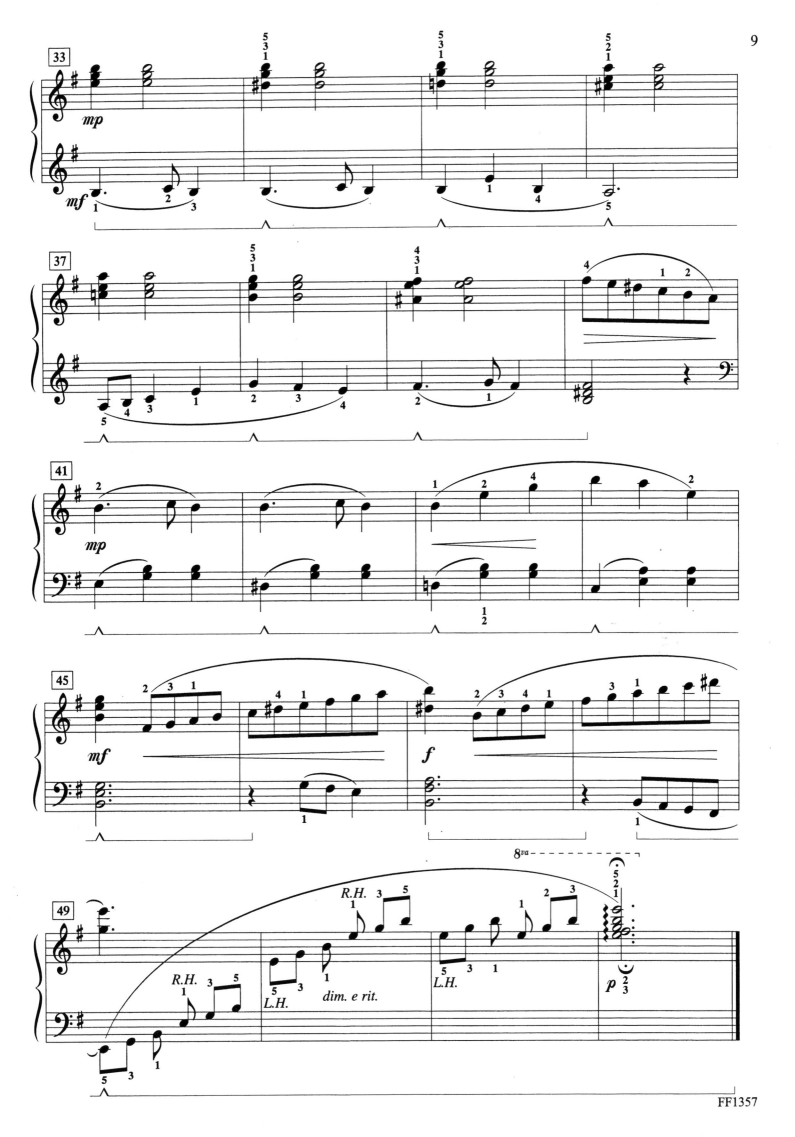

Autumn Skies

A Moment in Time

14

Moonlit Garden

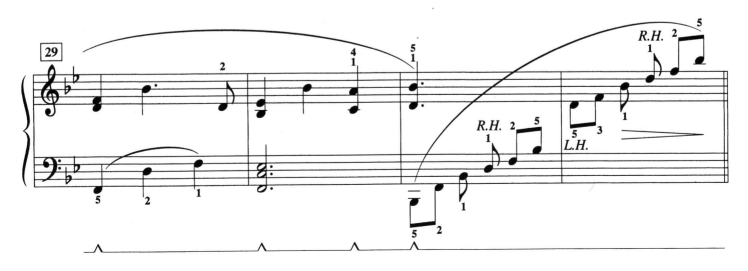

FF1357

The Sweetest of Dreams

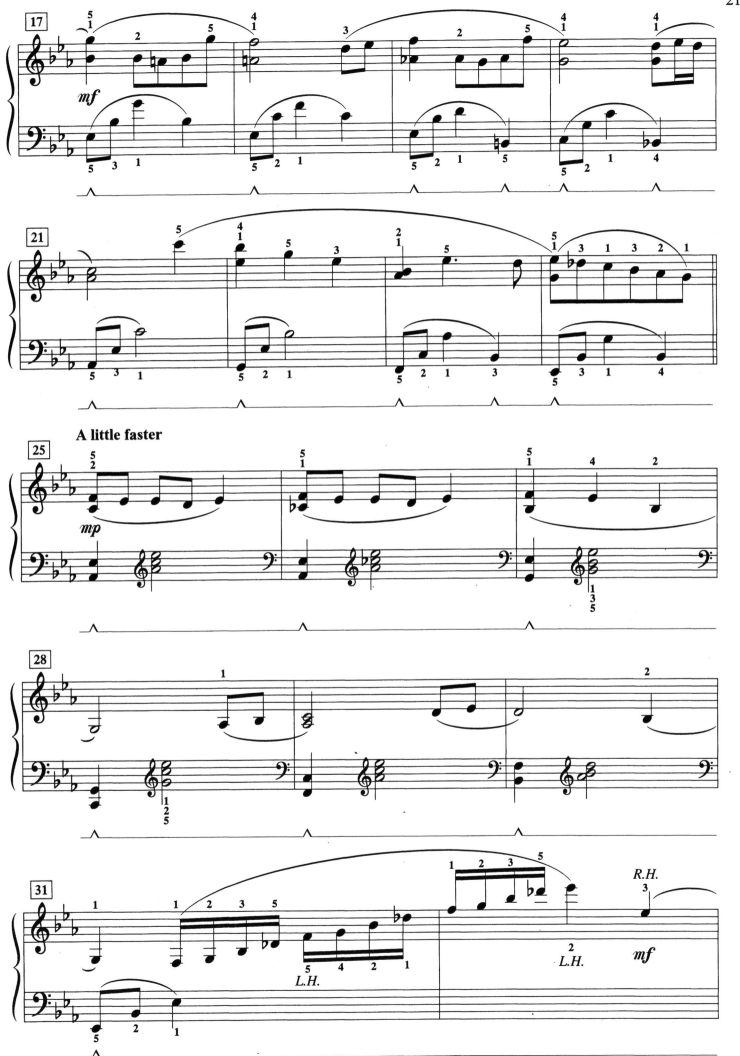

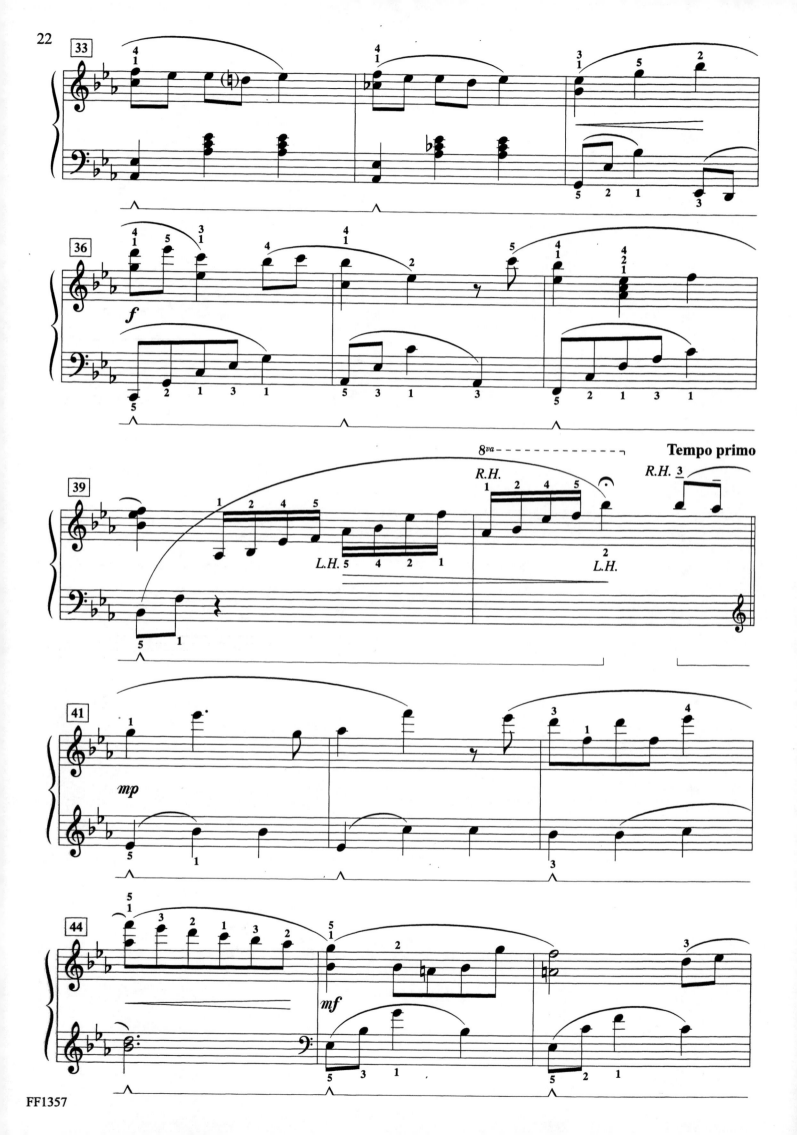

A Magical Night

With anticipation ($\quad$ = ca. 96)